Little Houses

COLORING BOOK

By SAMED 87

Al l Rights Reserved 2020

Copyright Material

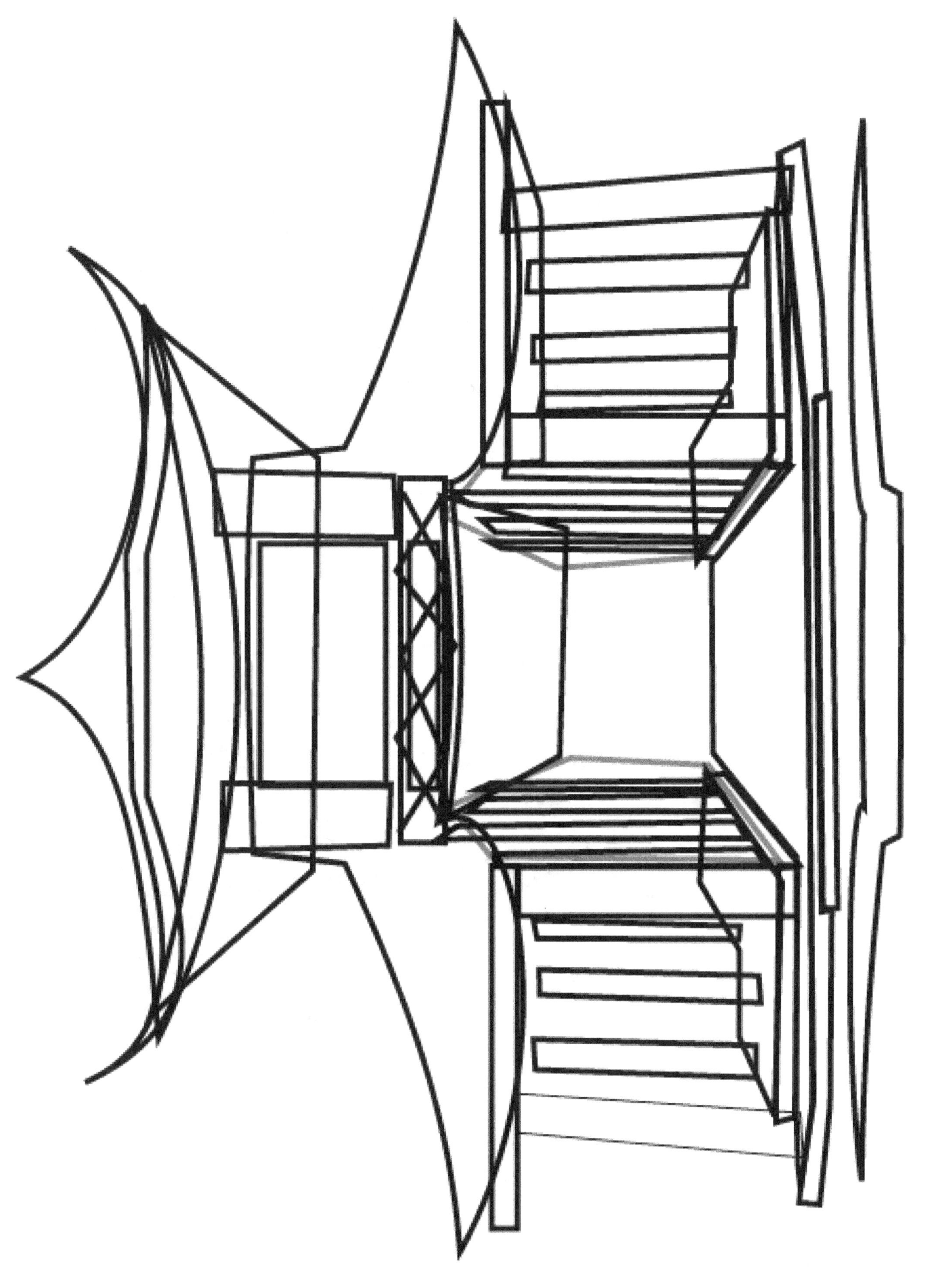

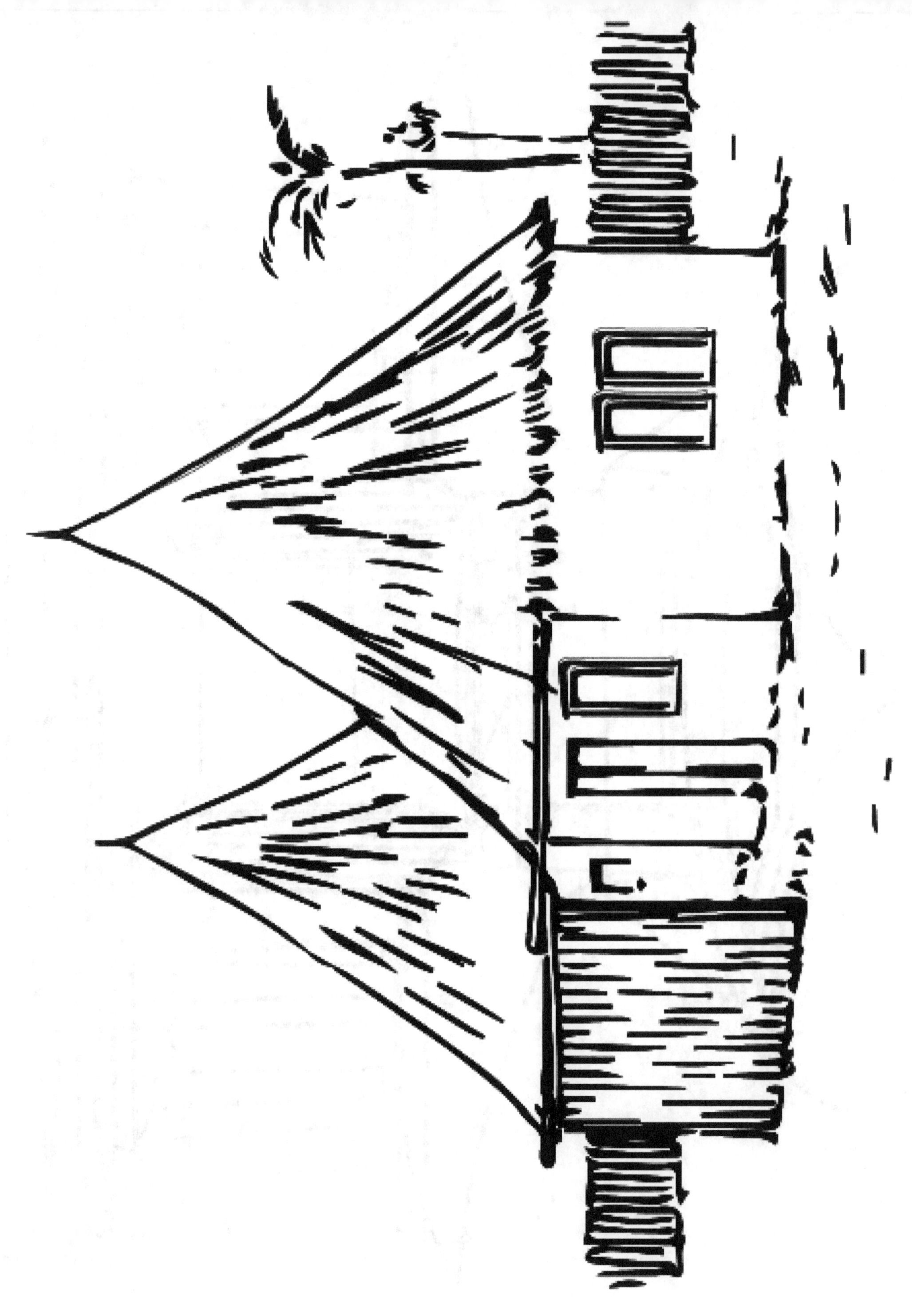

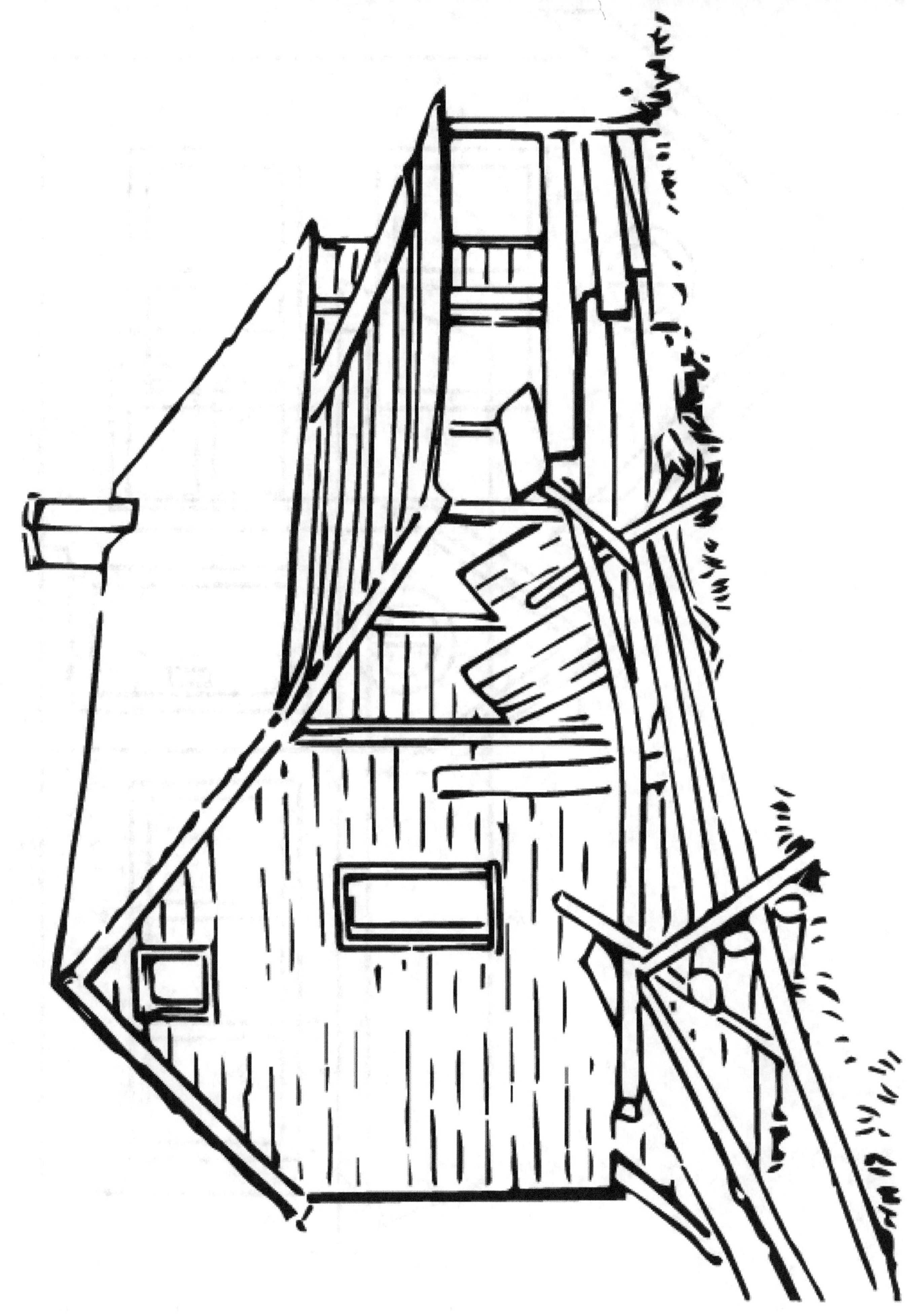

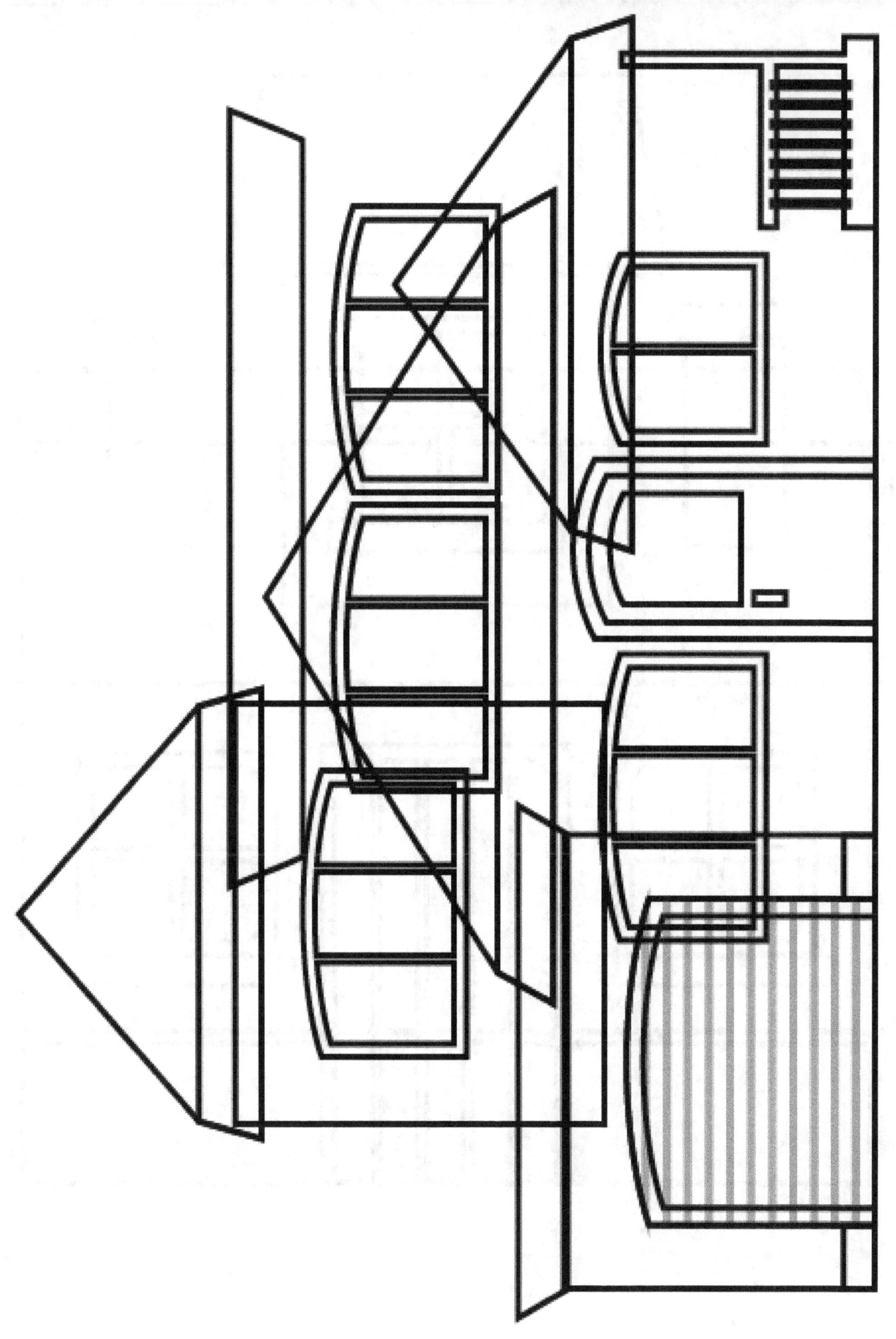

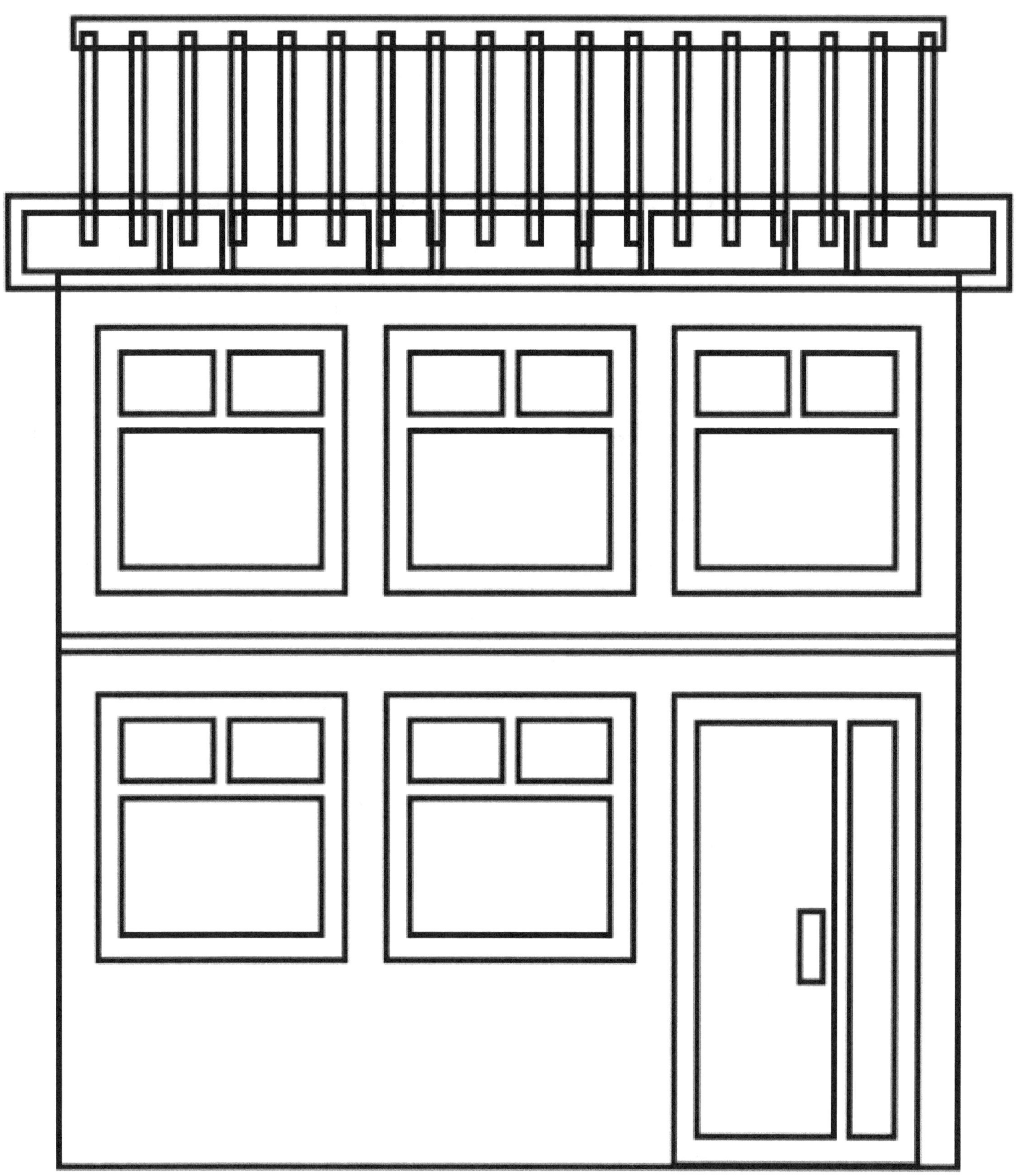

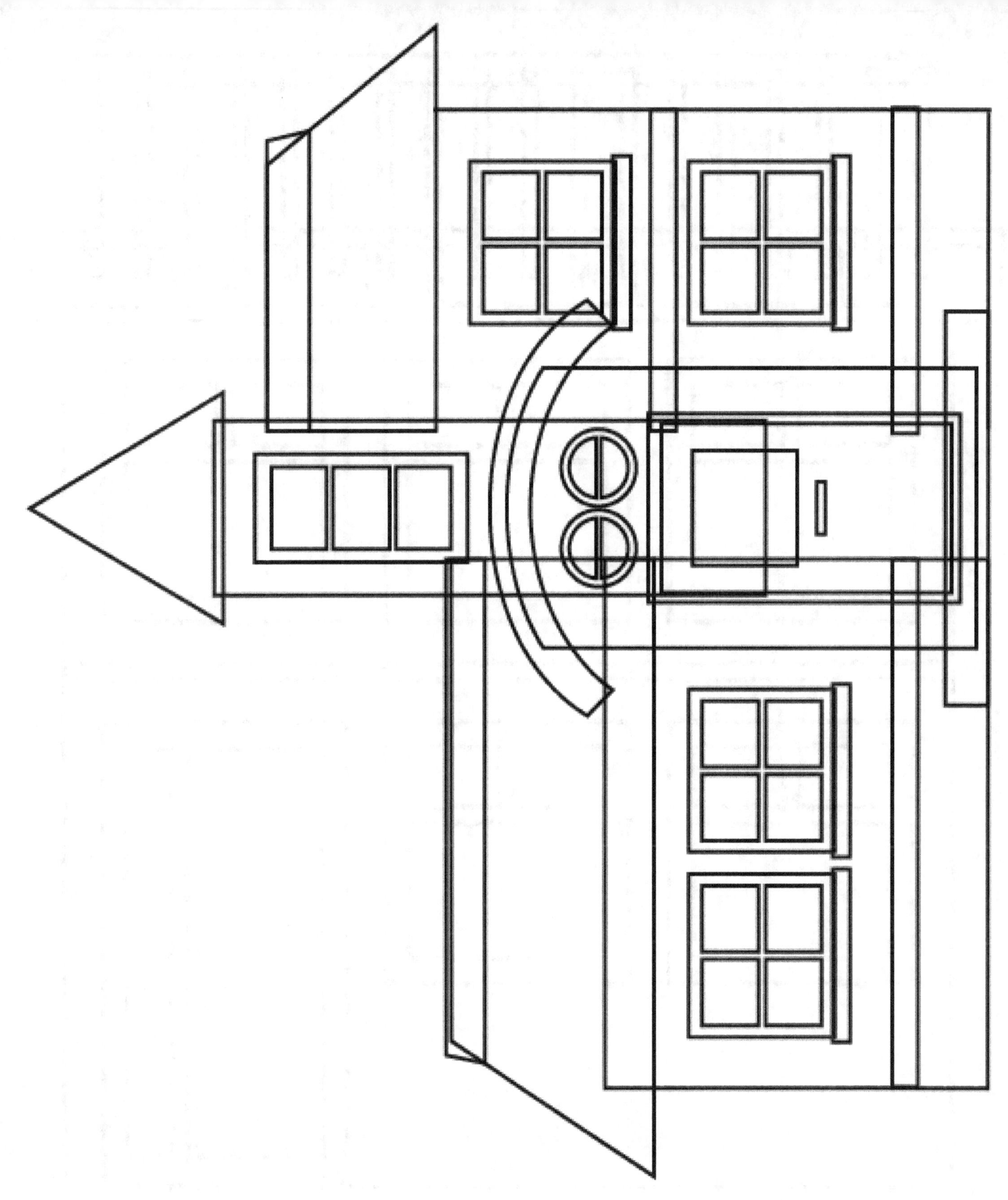

Copyright Material

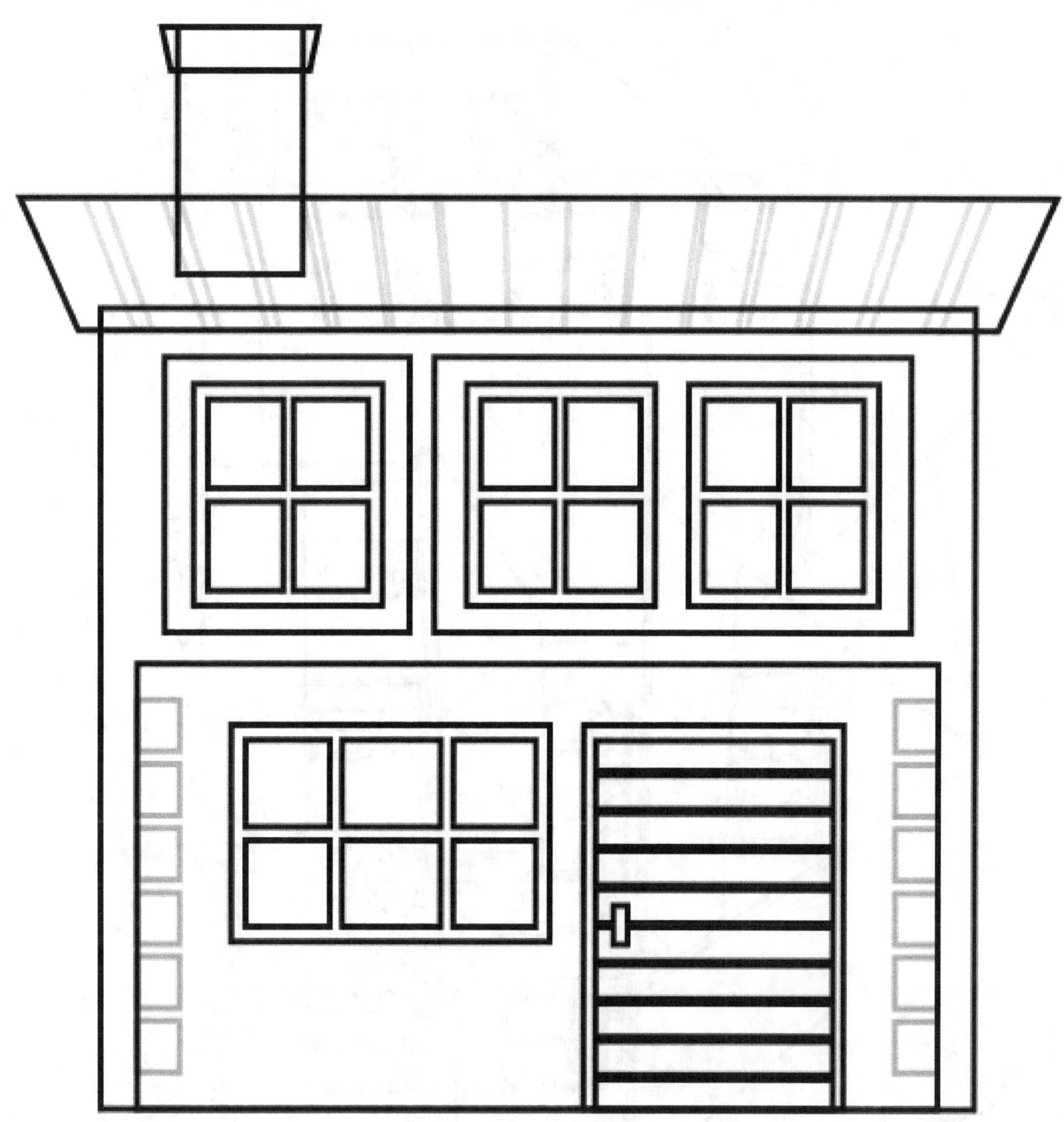

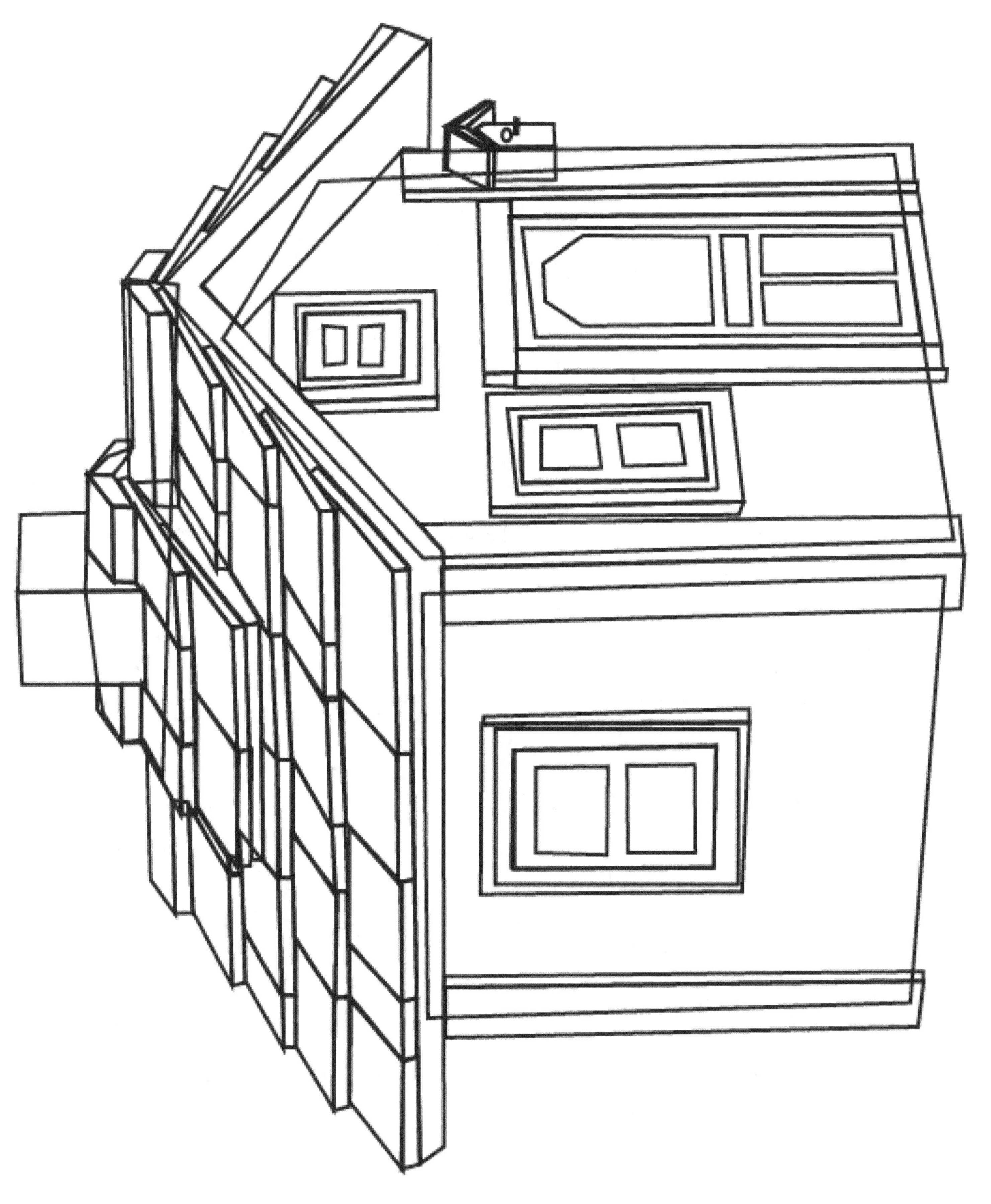

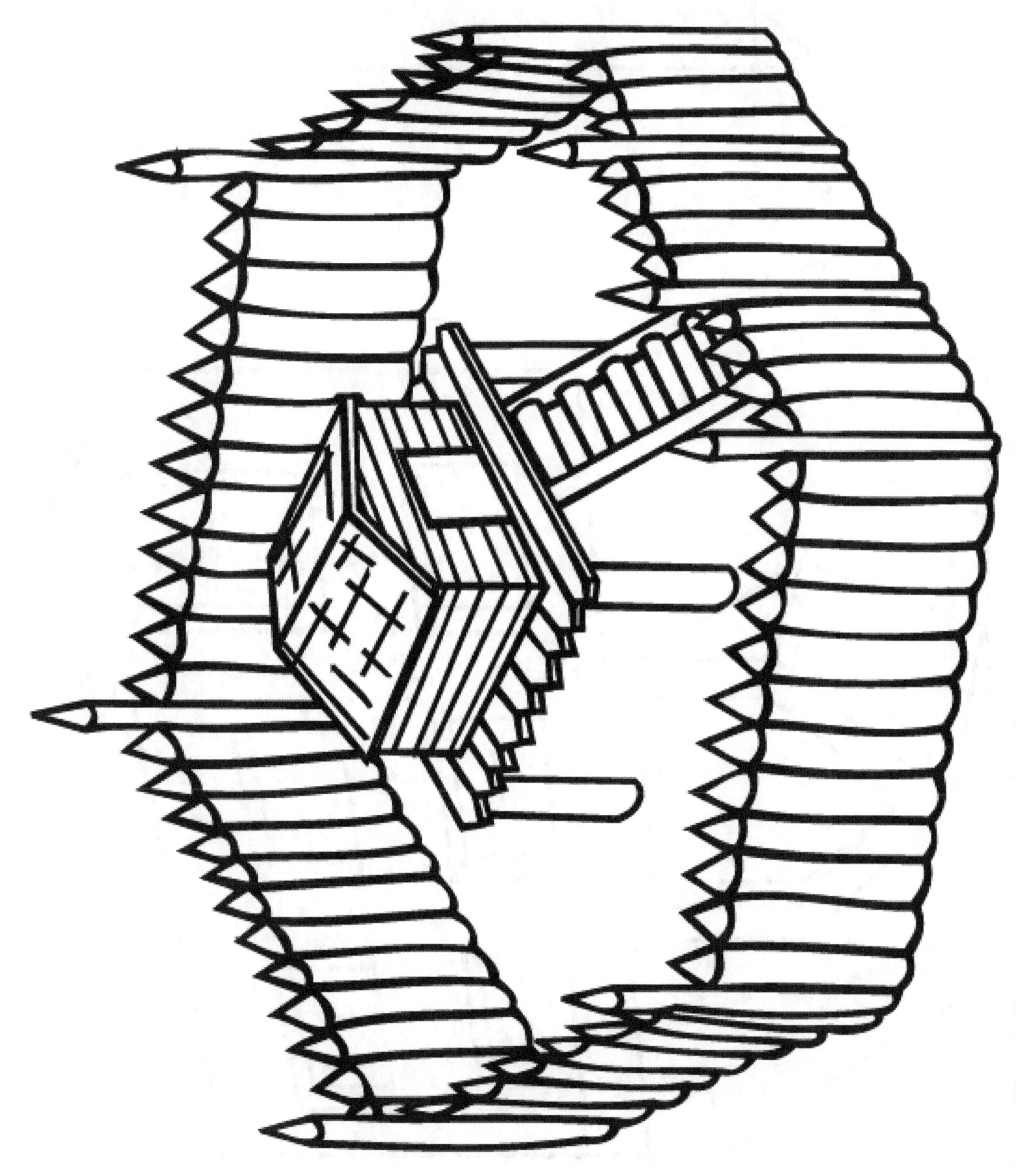

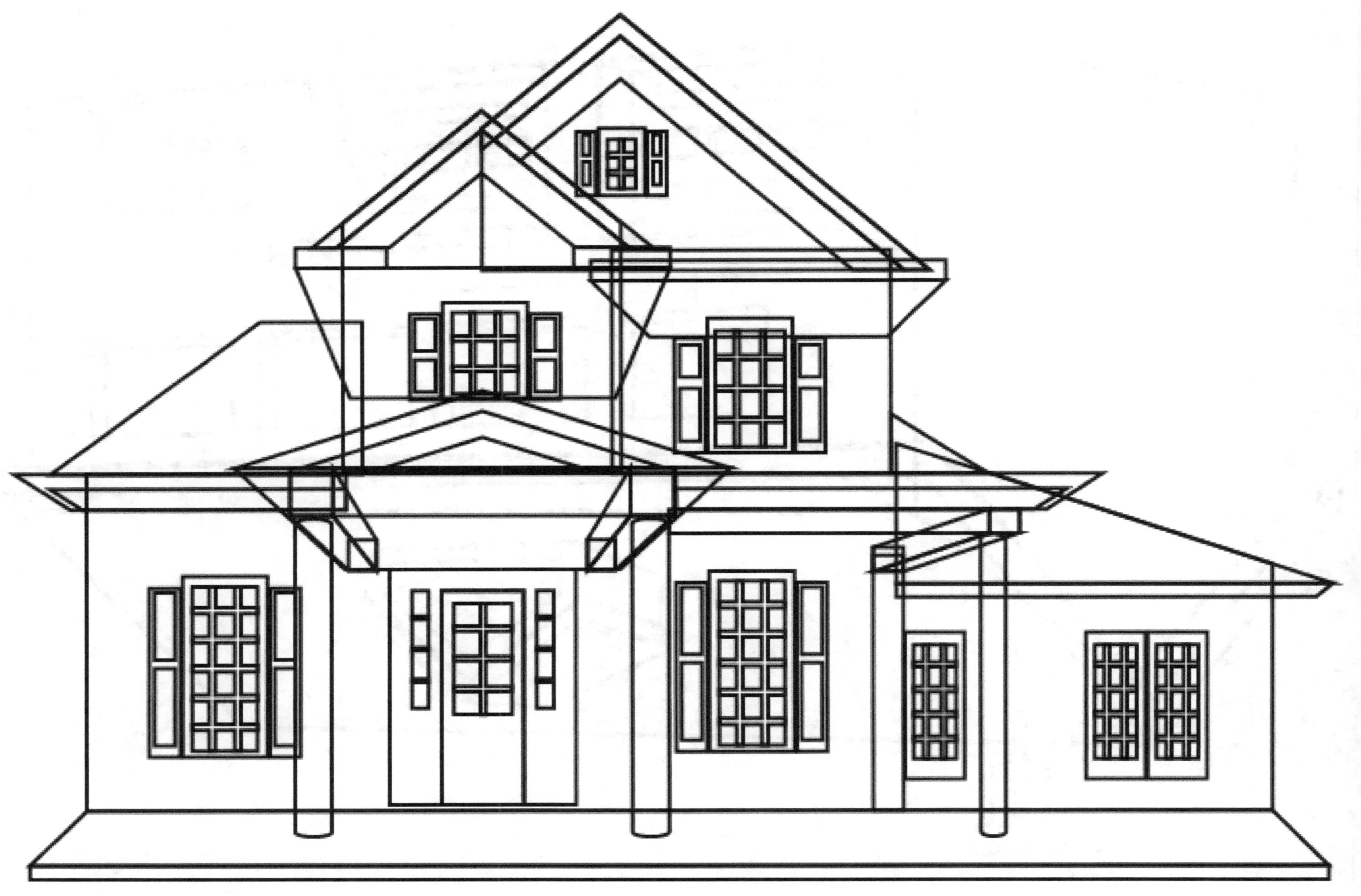

Copyright Material

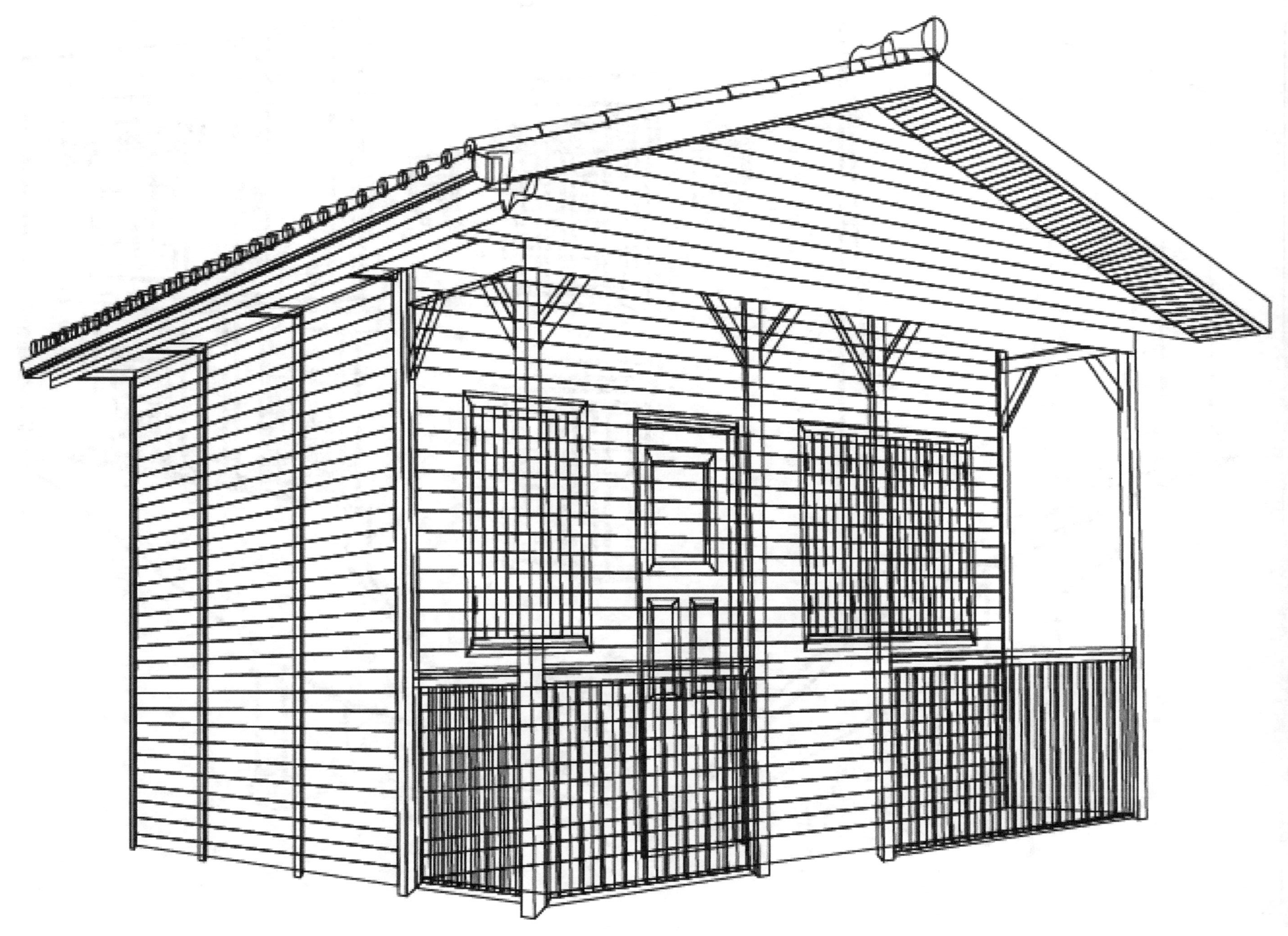

Copyright Material

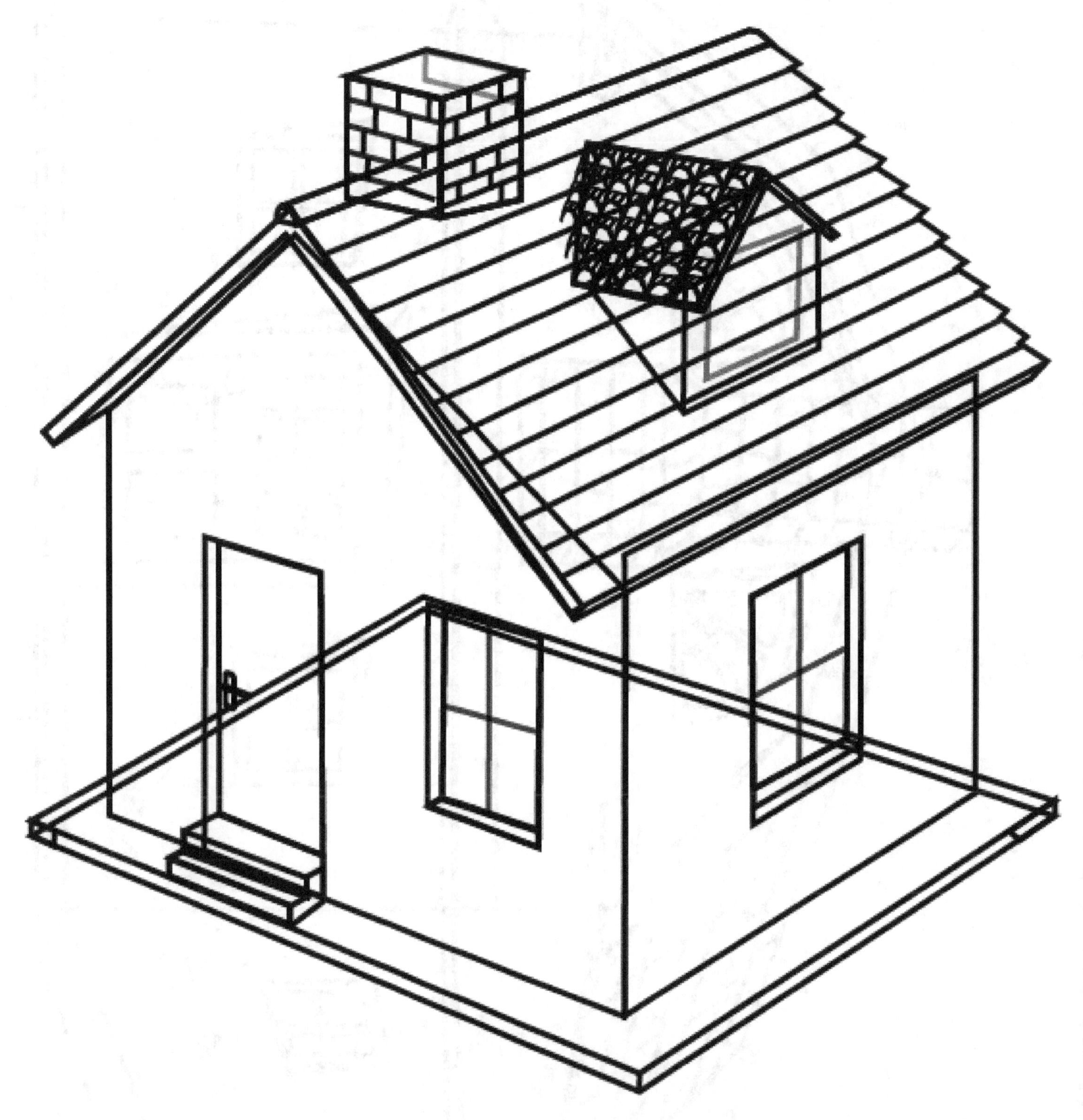

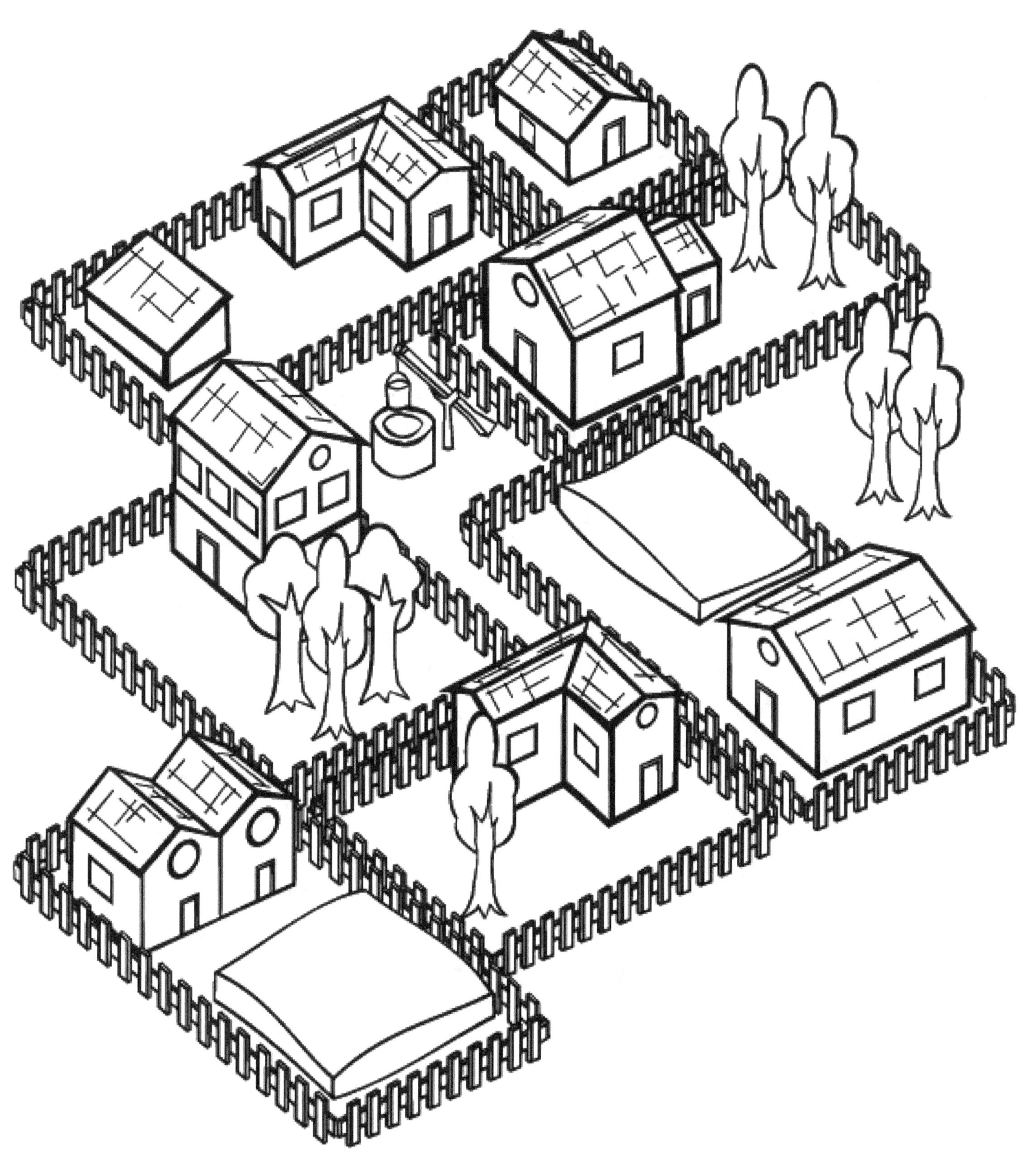

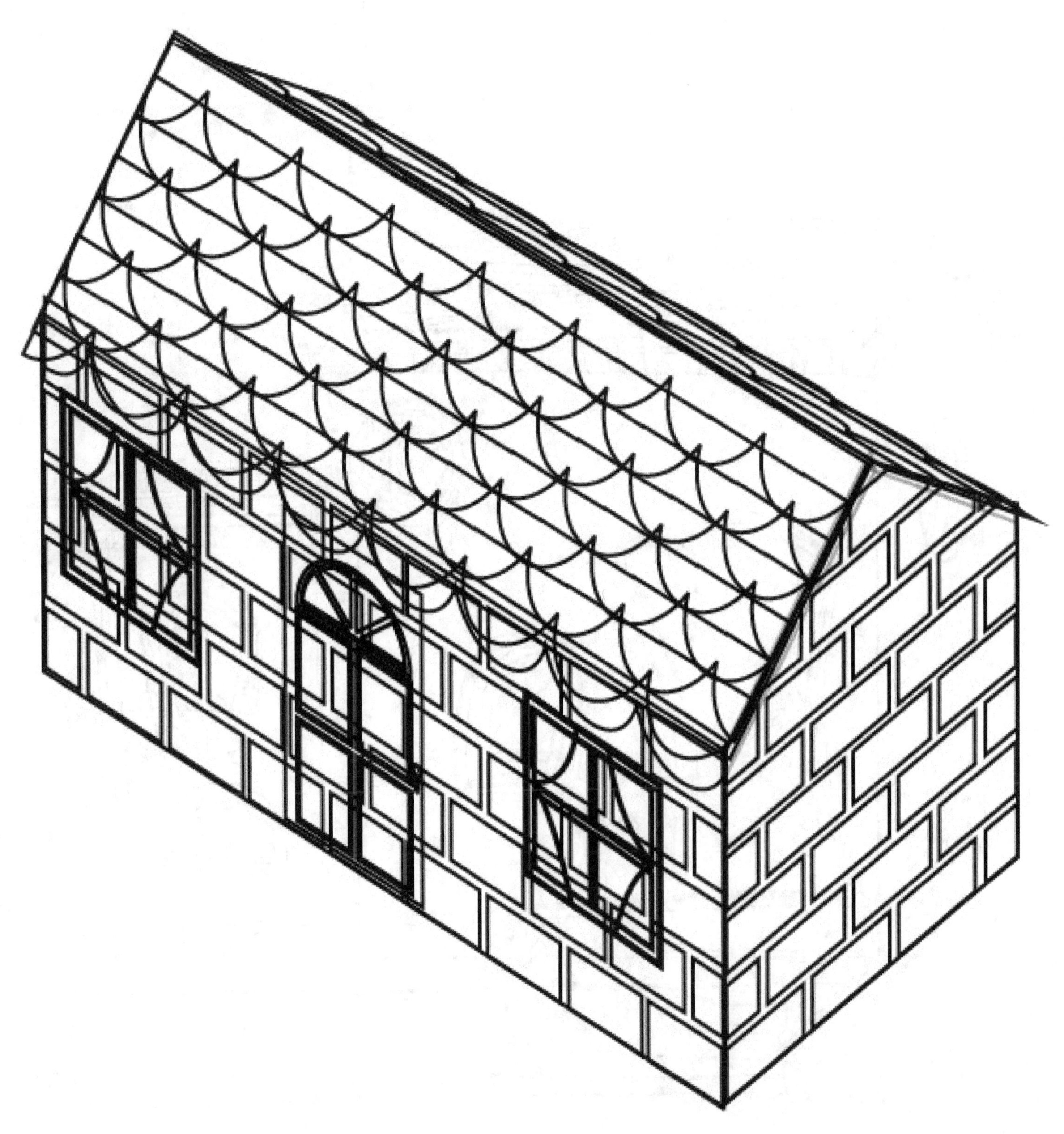

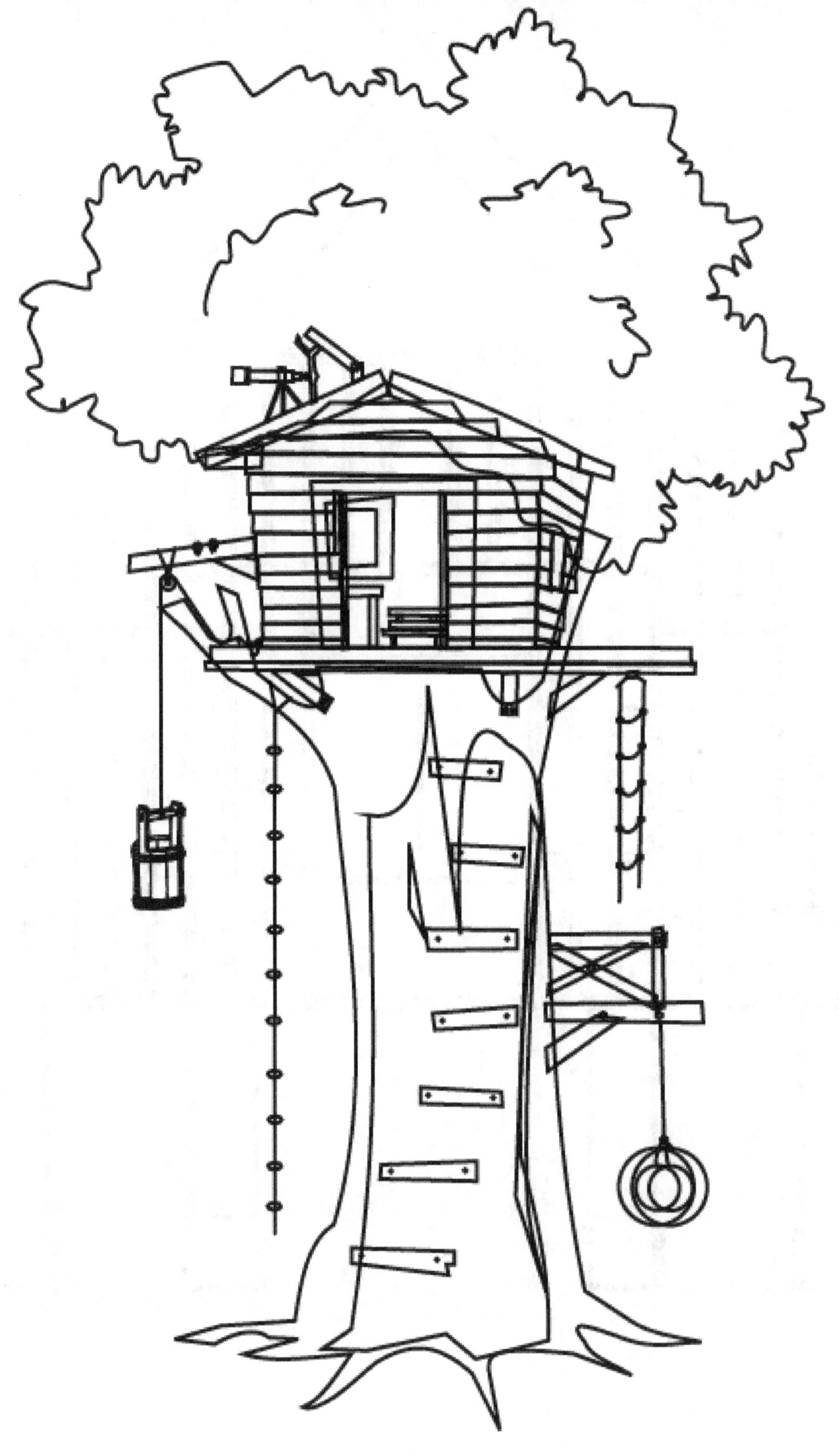

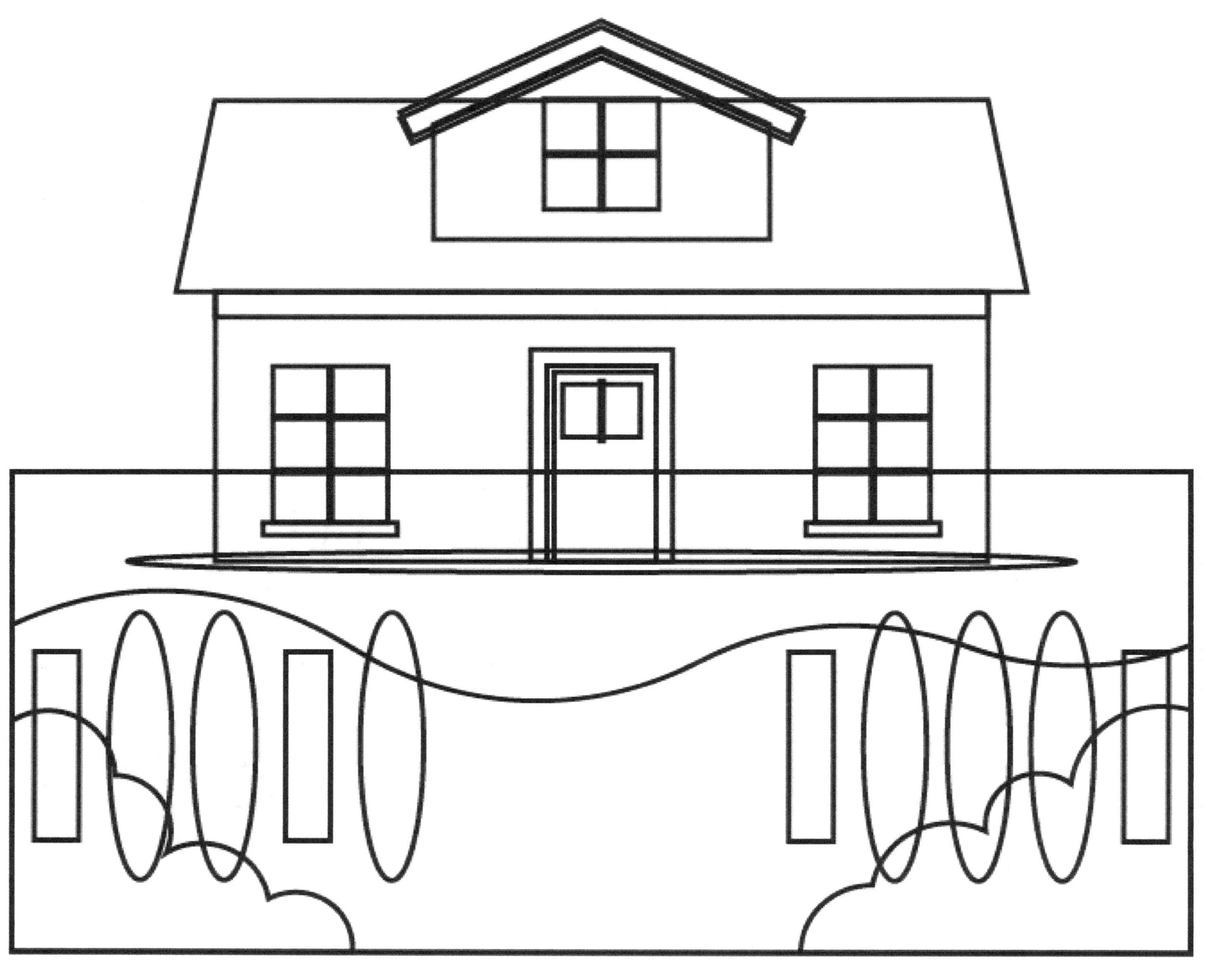

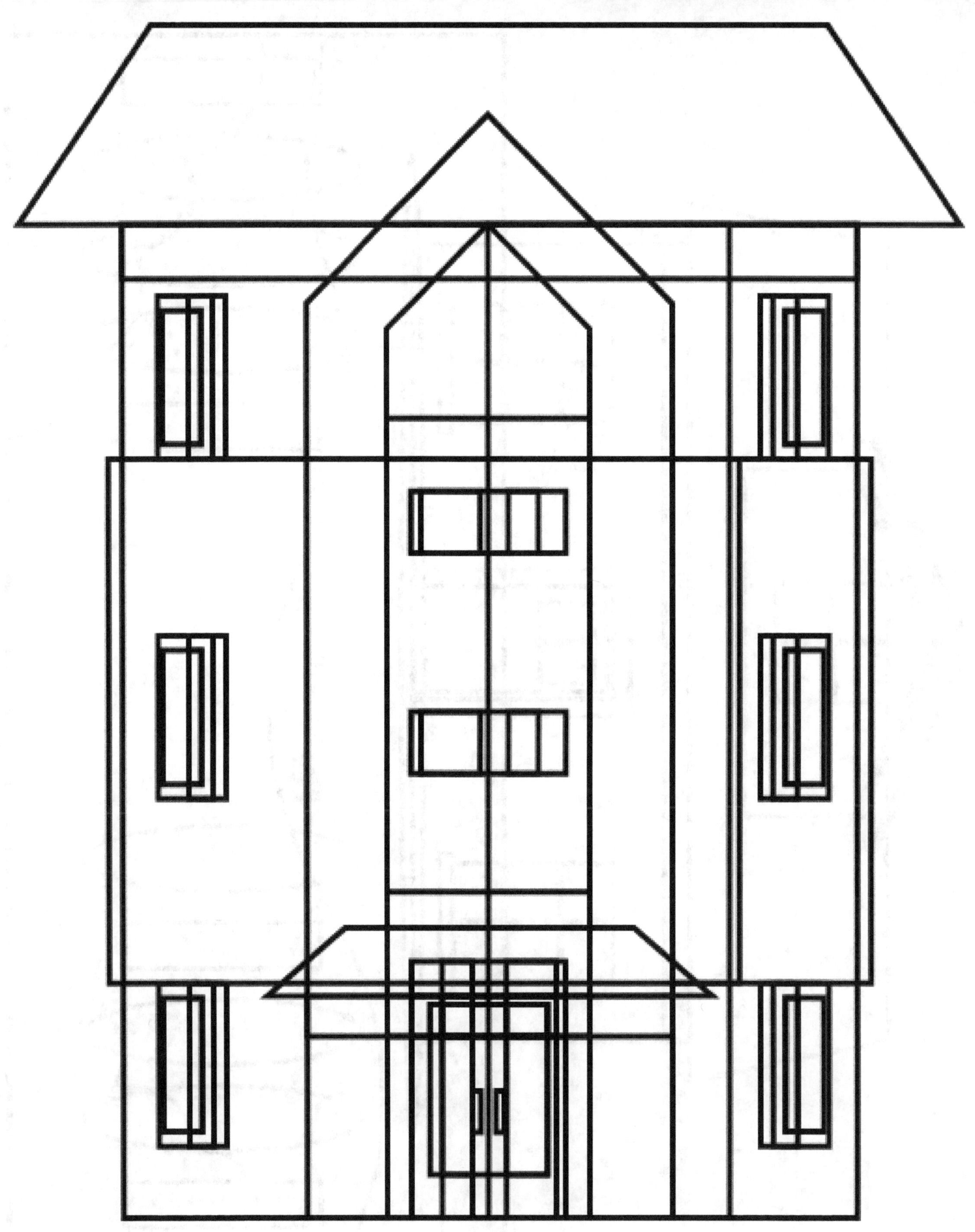

Copyright Material

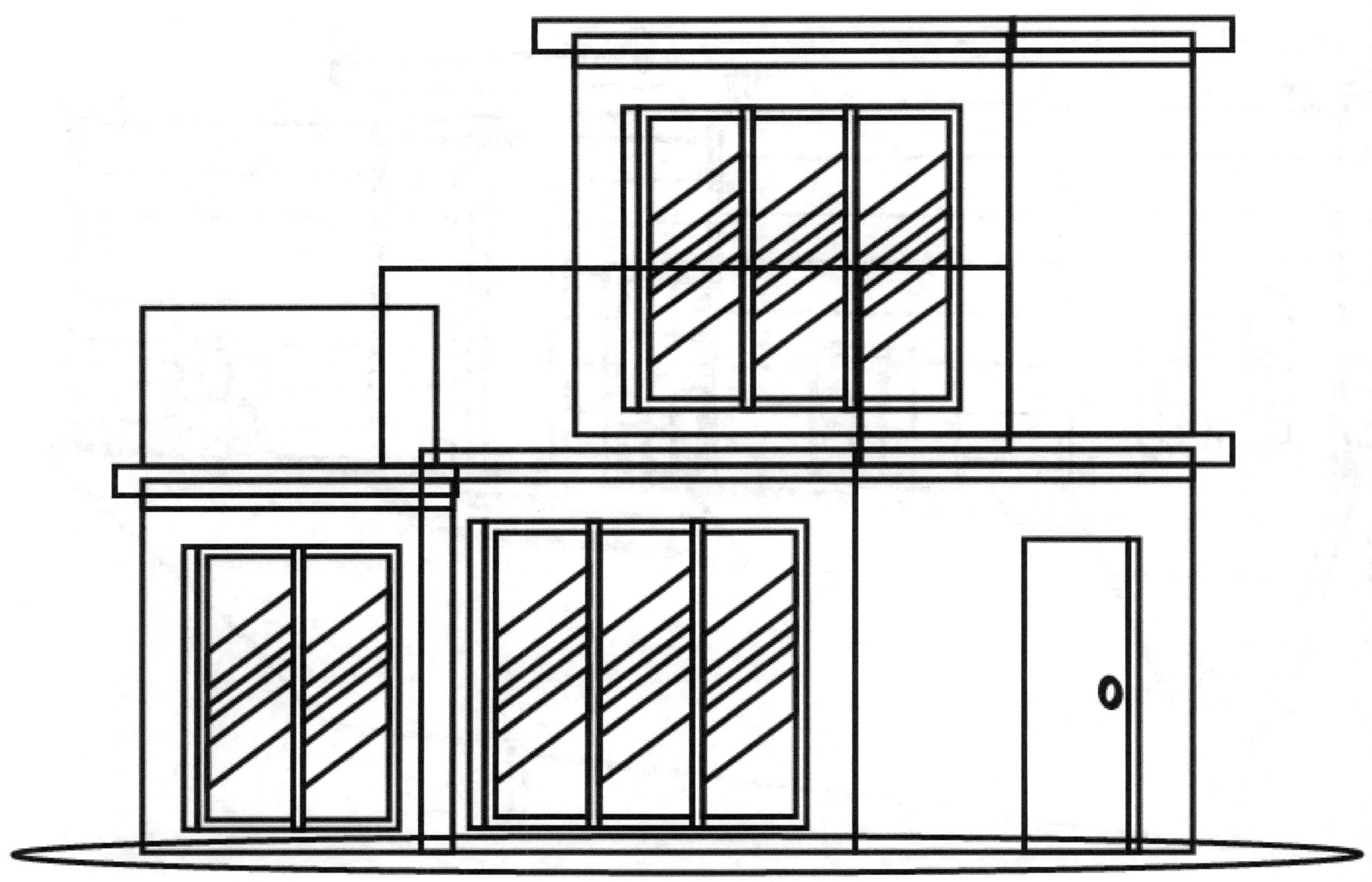

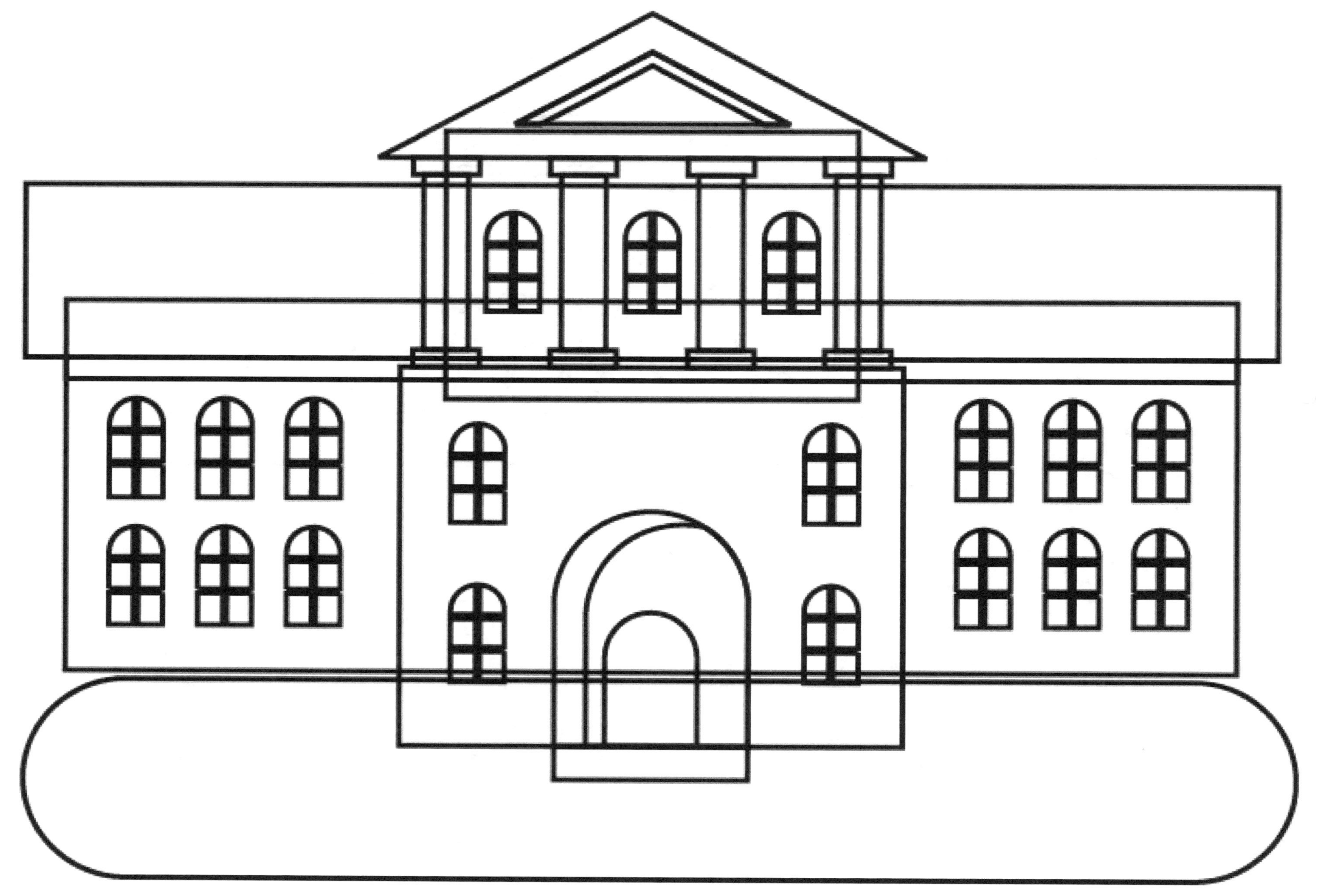

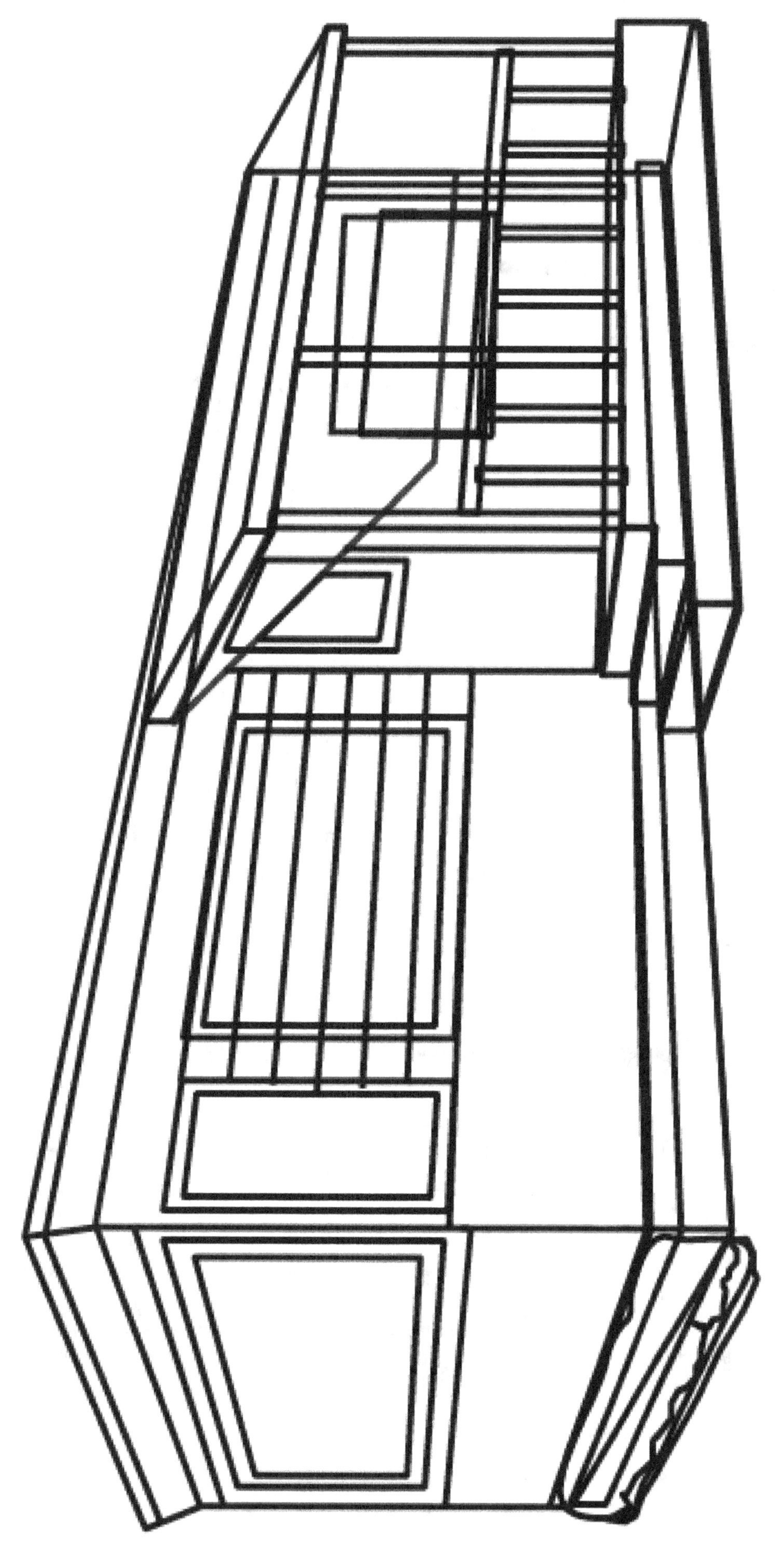

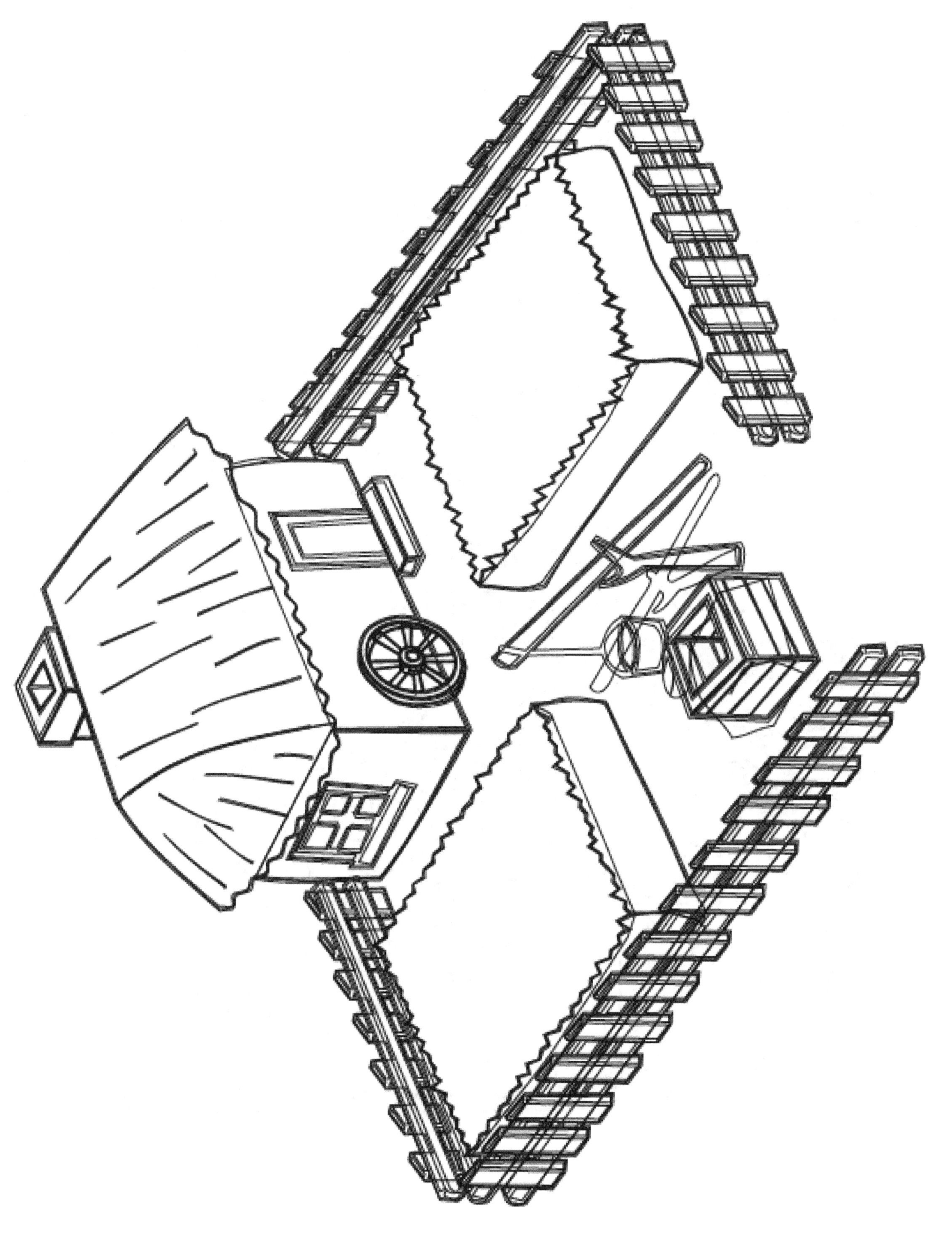